M000267205

A Man's
Late Night Thoughts

J. Richman

DORRANCE
PUBLISHING CO
EST. 1920
PITTSBURGH, PENNSYLVANIA 15238

The contents of this work, including, but not limited to, the accuracy of events, people, and places depicted; opinions expressed; permission to use previously published materials included; and any advice given or actions advocated are solely the responsibility of the author, who assumes all liability for said work and indemnifies the publisher against any claims stemming from publication of the work.

All Rights Reserved
Copyright © 2019 by J. Richman

No part of this book may be reproduced or transmitted, downloaded, distributed, reverse engineered, or stored in or introduced into any information storage and retrieval system, in any form or by any means, including photocopying and recording, whether electronic or mechanical, now known or hereinafter invented without permission in writing from the publisher.

Dorrance Publishing Co
585 Alpha Drive
Suite 103
Pittsburgh, PA 15238
Visit our website at *www.dorrancebookstore.com*

ISBN: 978-1-6453-0130-1
eISBN: 978-1-6453-0957-4

Prologue

These original thoughts and insights were written by me over many years.

Perhaps it is fear of rejection or it seemed as unmanly for most men to say to family, friends or the world—this is me.

I wish someone had written this book 100 years ago and I had been compelled to study as a boy on my way though the teen ages.

To ladies of all ages——
These thoughts will pertain to your life too.
You may say I did not know I knew this until I read it.
 If there a man in your life father—son—husband—friend—-
This is a short cut to understanding them.

To the men——
You will know you are not alone—
Some thoughts will make you smile others—long sought after relief some sad reflections but perhaps closure to unfinished business.

A perfect gift to—anyone you care about.

◦◦◦

problems accrue when we
confuse how a woman looks
with who she is

Your Comments

by J. Richman

∾∾∾

if I had a party and invited the
different me of different ages
there would much argument
perhaps a fight or two

_____

Your Comments

by J. Richman

❧

what happens when we sit down
with ourselves and ask
is this what I had in mind for me
is the answer ever yes

Your Comments

∾∾∾

what happens when unimportant me
wants to be important

Your Comments

by J. Richman

∾∾∾

can this me
find a better me

Your Comments

by J. Richman

∽∾∽

introspection requires us to be
an interested spectator
of our own life

Your Comments

by J. Richman

༄༅

can anyone understand us
and
love us anyway

_____

Your Comments

by J. Richman

༄

can anyone roam about those
dark protected areas
of my mind without thinking
I am crazy

_____

Your Comments

⌒⌒⌒

why must we clutch
desperately
to our fantasy

Your Comments

by J. Richman

❦

great chemistry is pure pain
then one you want
doesn't share your dreams

_____

Your Comments

by J. Richman

∾∾

there are one million ways
to kill off the soft loving parts
of ourselves and others
how many do you know

_____

Your Comments

by J. Richman

∾∾∾

how many dreams can crap out
before part of us crap out too

_____

Your Comments

by J. Richman

⤫⤫⤫

for reason I don't fully understand
I don't fully understand anything

_____

Your Comments

by J. Richman

the world has bent me more
than I have bent it

_____

Your Comments

by J. Richman

∽⌒∾

be careful
we all have a extraordinary capacity
for self-deception

_____

Your Comments

15

∾

do you require all
to be dishonest with you
as you would twist their truth and
use it against them

Your Comments

❧

it's important that our vision
out see our sight

———————————————————————

Your Comments

17

by J. Richman

∽∾

what would you do
if you were forced
to give up boredom

_____

Your Comments

18

⌒⌒⌒

now and then
losing yourself and
feeling only the moment
a worthy goal

Your Comments

⤳⤳

is hell still down deep
in the earth or have
you relocated it

_____

Your Comments

by J. Richman

⚜

the atheist
the religious
one open
one closed
which is which

_____

Your Comments

by J. Richman

∽∾∽

some people must keep pets
so they can touch and
feel some love

_____

Your Comments

by J. Richman

❧

question
are we running from something
or to something

Your Comments

by J. Richman

◡◠◡

what happens when we need more
from life than is available

Your Comments

by J. Richman

do you frolic and run with the deer
in deer hunting season

Your Comments

by J. Richman

❧

how long can you
befriend both
the fox and the hounds

_____

Your Comments

by J. Richman

❧

not to worry
it's all in the grand plan
that you can change anytime

Your Comments

⌁⌁⌁

given my life's give and takes
oddly I wake every day
Happy—a new adventure

_____

Your Comments

by J. Richman

❧

too often my logical mind
and my emotional mind
are hostile enemies

_____

Your Comments

29

✂︎

a friendly smile
is like a warm gentle wind
that warms everything in its path

_____

Your Comments

30

by J. Richman

❧

for a while
it's understandable to require
your new loved one to be close by
and in sight
after a while it's crazy

_____

Your Comments

31

⌒⌒⌒

do you believe in happy endings
why

Your Comments

by J. Richman

ᵔᵔᵔ

the toughest lesson
love is never enough

_____

Your Comments

by J. Richman

∾∾∿

loving you is like
trying
embracing smoke

_____

Your Comments

by J. Richman

❧

holding on to anger
is like holding on to
a rope, pulling you into the abysses
save yourself
let go!!!

Your Comments

by J. Richman

remember
everyone does what
they think at the time
is in their best interest

Your Comments

by J. Richman

૭൞ഩ

intellectually I understand
it's your right,
however emotionally
you're driving me fxxkxx crazy!!!

_____

Your Comments

by J. Richman

❦

mutuality of interest the
key to all relationships

_____

Your Comments

by J. Richman

⌒⌒⌒

first consider
the source of every problem
then
surprise everybody react appropriately

Your Comments

by J. Richman

∾᷈

you can feel it before
you know or express
she changing slowly
and in time gone
the lost will remain

Your Comments

by J. Richman

❧❧

the above she can be
changed to—-a he

_____

Your Comments

by J. Richman

～～

memory is related
to truth
but not its twin

Your Comments

by J. Richman

❧

new romantic love
the connection between
a calm hot bath
and pure panic

Your Comments

by J. Richman

〜〜〜

will you go on expecting
a weapon
in every empty hand

Your Comments

by J. Richman

❧

sometimes we all do
things that only
fit in a nightmare

Your Comments

by J. Richman

∾⌒∾

the joy has faded
and I miss
the fantasy of you

Your Comments

by J. Richman

❧

are your love memories
nothing more
than a book you have read
and put away

Your Comments

by J. Richman

⌒⌒⌒

some switch between
love and hate
like an drunk

Your Comments

by J. Richman

∽∼∽

it's easy to die for our children
the trick is to live with them

_____

Your Comments

❦

there are times we all cry in private
as the victims
in our own Greek tragedy

_____

Your Comments

by J. Richman

∾∾

if it was meant to be
why isn't it

_____

Your Comments

by J. Richman

how many of our possible
alternative
futures do we preclude

Your Comments

by J. Richman

∾∾

why are some so
damm insensitive
to the pain in their wake

Your Comments

by J. Richman

⌒⌒⌒

even if you use both legs
you can't outrun your vision

_____

Your Comments

by J. Richman

⤫

you felt the hand of faith pressing
your new love against you
then why this storm

_____

Your Comments

by J. Richman

∽∾∽

marriage,
my life always a good concept
yet unpracticed those I loved
or me

Your Comments

by J. Richman

∾∾

who are you now
who will you be next
a fair question for
those of us that
change a lot

Your Comments

by J. Richman

how does this old-fashioned man
reinvent himself to fit the
future history of the 21st century

Your Comments

by J. Richman

❦

there is this flame of your
fantasy deep inside me
but there are times
I can't handle your
cold reality

Your Comments

by J. Richman

❧

exploitation of another
depreciates both parties

Your Comments

by J. Richman

how big is the leap
between your truth
and your hope

Your Comments

by J. Richman

❧

can anyone but me
peel away my layers
of disappointment

Your Comments

by J. Richman

ᔕᔕᔕ

question
just how subjective
is our personal truth

Your Comments

by J. Richman

⌒⌒

if you knew that you truly believe
you wouldn't torture yourself
week after week—well unless

Your Comments

by J. Richman

❀

hmmmmm
true believers instruction for
branding your slaves can be
found in the old Testament

Your Comments

65

❦

don't worry yourself out
of a good life

_____

Your Comments

by J. Richman

❧❧❧

what happens inside you when you
hurt someone and know better

_____

Your Comments

by J. Richman

ᕲᕲᕲ

so far there has been only one woman
I really wanted to hold
all through the night
but she is all but gone now

Your Comments

by J. Richman

⌘

There is this sadness

Your Comments

by J. Richman

∾∾

Silly me
I have a profound
need for the warmth,
healing and understanding that comes
with the intimacy of love

_____

Your Comments

by J. Richman

⌘

marriage
a bright abstraction I aimed for
our life always fore evermore
now that's out of style

_____

Your Comments

by J. Richman

❦

best to know if our fears
are a creation
of our fantasy or our reality

_____

Your Comments

by J. Richman

❧

sometimes
it's really tough being really me

_____

Your Comments

by J. Richman

∽∾∿

can I unwound you
can you unwound me

_____

Your Comments

by J. Richman

∿∿

remember this
mother nature's priority
system really works
if something or someone
becomes important
you will find the time

Your Comments

75

꙳꙳

where am I supposed to be
there was a time I knew

Your Comments

by J. Richman

~⌒~

much too late a love warns me
I will be the worst thing that ever
happens to you
question
why did she have to prove it

_____

Your Comments

by J. Richman

༼ຎຎ༽

self-destruction seeps up
out of the blackness
of you, my love

Your Comments

by J. Richman

⌘

it is really interesting
when our fantasies
bump into realities

_____

Your Comments

by J. Richman

◦◦◦

life after death
"how convenient"

_____

Your Comments

by J. Richman

∽∼∽

don't kid yourself
we are all bigots
it's just a question of degree

_____

Your Comments

by J. Richman

❧

ever wish there was
someone else
in the other room

_____

Your Comments

by J. Richman

most lives are a questionable balance
of our instincts and religious dogmas

Your Comments

by J. Richman

c??????

overtime
how many former lovers
are too many

Your Comments

by J. Richman

❦

how much of me
can I give up to
be with a new love

Your Comments

by J. Richman

there are times everyone views
life as a moving train
stuck on a track to oblivion

_____

Your Comments

by J. Richman

⤜⤐⤍

keep changing your
life until one morning
you wake up and say
" Oh goody another day"

Your Comments

by J. Richman

❡

am I nothing more
than a crutch to lean on
where my crutch

_____

Your Comments

by J. Richman

⌘

overwhelmed or under whelmed
to trick is not to
be whelmed at all

_____

Your Comments

by J. Richman

◟◞◟◞

personal integrity is to great of
a burden for me to be an attorney,
politician or _____

_____

Your Comments

by J. Richman

we must learn
to be strong enough
to be gentle

_____

Your Comments

❧

a true home is a safe place where
we are welcome
even when we are wrong

Your Comments

by J. Richman

if your house burns down
you have only lost a place
to put your home in

_____

Your Comments

∽∾∾

my diary
History and insights
from the inner me
overtime to
the future me
little is forgotten
much is learned

_____

Your Comments

by J. Richman

⌒⌒⌒

when reminded by others
of past mistakes
just reply how unkind
of you to recall that

Your Comments

by J. Richman

꒰ꇁꇁ꒱

point of view
sometimes we need
new one from floor up

Your Comments

by J. Richman

∽∾∾

it's best we list our greatest
assets to give us strength
to carry the cross with which
we all burdened ourselves

Your Comments

by J. Richman

◦◦◦

is there such a thing as
"just" being a woman
or "just" being a man

_____

Your Comments

by J. Richman

⤮

heaven
will you be driven
to change it too

_____

Your Comments

by J. Richman

❦

inappropriate
A great word to describe many
friends, former lovers and most
my candidates for marriage

_____

Your Comments

❧❧

overtime
BRASH people become
cartoons of themselves

_____

Your Comments

by J. Richman

⌒⌒⌒

genes and intelligence earned
through eons
now flow to my children and
now beyond them"cool"

Your Comments

by J. Richman

❧

THERE ARE THOSE WHO WOULD RAGE EVEN AGAINST THEIR ECHO

Your Comments

by J. Richman

problems occur when
we confuse
how women look
with who they are

_____

Your Comments

104

∽∾∽

it is just me and my wife
now and the little one—
her Iphone that I share
equal time with

_____

Your Comments

by J. Richman

❧

could it be for some
we are nothing more than a
financial security blanket

Your Comments

by J. Richman

❧

goodbye note on my pillow
it's like I'm gray and you're white
I painted me white
but it's rubbing off

Your Comments

by J. Richman

⤯⤯⤯

a great retort
I said how are you
she smiled
and said "deelicious"

———————————————————————

Your Comments

by J. Richman

୶୶୶

our explanations
are seldom
our reasons

_____

Your Comments

by J. Richman

I have shed more tears
from pain than joy

_____

Your Comments

by J. Richman

∽◦∽

true leaders are only actors
when they have to follow

_____

Your Comments

by J. Richman

❦

strange available women chase
unavailable men
stranger yet is why any available
chases any unavailable

Your Comments

by J. Richman

❤❤❤

how is it some people have both
unlimited enthusiasm
and unlimited problems

_____

Your Comments

113

⚘

sometimes it's difficult to see beyond
the wreckage of our lives
but we must!
take heart!
we are more than our mistakes

Your Comments

by J. Richman

∽⌒∽

I have yet to find
the right woman
at right time
for all time

Your Comments

by J. Richman

❦

over 60
the road ahead is shorter
than the one behind

Your Comments

∽∾∾

if someone gives you a guilt trip
don't go

_____

Your Comments

by J. Richman

∽∾∽

it can be a curse to understand
the great things
you could've done

_____

Your Comments

by J. Richman

❧

good insight
is required in order to
have good foresight

Your Comments

by J. Richman

ↄ∾ↄ

I don't even have
20/20
hindsight

Your Comments

by J. Richman

∽∾∽

the reason we fall in love with
flawed people is that
that's the only kind of
people there are

Your Comments

by J. Richman

∽◡∾

more to come

_____

Your Comments

by J. Richman

∽∽

who would want
"touched the world lightly"
over their gravestone

Your Comments

by J. Richman

❦

most conscious decisions
are harder to make
than to live with

_____

Your Comments

124

❧~❧

why do some fight for every
extra moment in life
while others make death
threats against themselves

_____

Your Comments

guilt trips are not
required travel

Your Comments

by J. Richman

❧

all too often a sexually
acceptable lover is
socially unacceptable

Your Comments

by J. Richman

෴

true character often
intrudes into
true romance

_____

Your Comments

by J. Richman

‿︵‿

courtrooms are filled with
sanctimonious hypocrisy
with seats unavailable
for "fair or right"

Your Comments

by J. Richman

❦

I have loved many women
each in turn
made me feel like I
had never loved before

Your Comments

by J. Richman

∾∾

even people that give mature
consideration to their life act
immature from time to time

Your Comments

131

∽∾∾

I never tried drugs
as I knew if I liked them
I'd be screwed

Your Comments

❧

unconscious decisions are
often harder to live with

_____

Your Comments

by J. Richman

～～

unless we make ourselves
"available for" the good stuff
the only "stuff" will happen

_____

Your Comments

by J. Richman

❦

who you idolize is more about
you than them

_____

Your Comments

by J. Richman

❧❧

if you study the marriage vows
you'll understand a woman's needs

_____

Your Comments

by J. Richman

∾∾∾

bright and beautiful men and women
often lack nothing but the
ability to love and care

Your Comments

137

by J. Richman

ை௸

shared consequences is
a powerful incentive
in marriage
it is a necessity

_____

Your Comments

by J. Richman

❧

how do I explain to you or to me
that booze used by two of the ladies
of my life destroyed their lives
and altered my future

Your Comments

by J. Richman

∽∾∽

in human relationships
sometimes we need to
overlook both
the unforgivable
and unforgettable

Your Comments

140

⌒⌒

ladies think subterfuge
if he knows you'll chase him
you'll lose
worse yet, you'll get used

Your Comments

by J. Richman

❧

a man never worried about
she doesn't want the real me
just wants to use my body for
pleasure

Your Comments

࿊

some men have 50 women a year
but all wish for the right woman
for 50 years

Your Comments

by J. Richman

❧

not regretting a woman is a blessing
made better if mutual

_____

Your Comments

by J. Richman

⌒⌒

it's a true joy
When she improves my life
and we know it

_____

Your Comments

by J. Richman

∽∾∾⌐

odd
too much beauty / brains
often lead to much pain

_____

Your Comments

146

by J. Richman

emotional vampires
are a problem
even if it's not Halloween

Your Comments

by J. Richman

ಬಾ

like a computer,
we must be upgradable,
to function over time

Your Comments

by J. Richman

letters state who
we want to be
actions give away
who we are

_____

Your Comments

149

～∾～

if your kids are to have
an indomitable spirit
It will be because you

Your Comments

by J. Richman

༺◦༻

think enough of yourself

to_____.

Your Comments

by J. Richman

෨෭෨

"now once again"
can be a very scary thought

Your Comments

by J. Richman

᚛᚜

blunt advice it is ill conceived
best to offer
a have you considered

Your Comments

⌒⌒

a test of friendships is
not in agreements
but in caring

_____

Your Comments

by J. Richman

only awareness can
protects you from
emotional vampires
lurking everywhere

Your Comments

by J. Richman

∽∾∽

search for consistency
find only inconsistency
time changes everything
every time

_____

Your Comments

by J. Richman

∾᷈᷈∾

serving an idol
would be a problem
droning is not my style

_____

Your Comments

by J. Richman

࿇

neat freaks can
have messy lives

Your Comments

by J. Richman

⌒⌒⌒

beware
messy home
messy mind

_____

Your Comments

by J. Richman

⌒⌒⌒

why have so many good women
really loved me
but I not them

_____

Your Comments

by J. Richman

❧

will your autobiography will be
about one adventure
after another don't bore
anyone that includes you

_____

Your Comments

by J. Richman

⌒⌒⌒

even if your song of life is
out of harmony
with others
don't let it be, unsung

_____

Your Comments

❧

everything is temporary
when understood
everything becomes more
important

_____

Your Comments

by J. Richman

∽∾∽

we are born without a mask
we erroneously construct one
required by our environment
and insecurities

Your Comments

by J. Richman

❧

unburdened by the weight
of the ice age
the earth reshapes itself
where's a message here
about the nature of all things

Your Comments

by J. Richman

☙～～❧

animals take less of us
to love than people

_____

Your Comments

by J. Richman

∽∼∽

change is more difficult
when shaped by known
past errors

_____

Your Comments

167

by J. Richman

❧

will there be a time when
my memories
exceed my expectations

Your Comments

by J. Richman

ᢳᢘᢲ

if you were required to act natural
what would you do

_____

Your Comments

by J. Richman

⮑✦⮐

some women are easy to love
but hard to like
then in time love dies

_____

Your Comments

170

⤭

I feel compelled to
resist the force of time
But I know it will not wait for long

Your Comments

171

∽∾∽

I must have purposes
in order to serve family
friends and myself

Your Comments

by J. Richman

be careful at what you succeed at
It could be worse than failure

Your Comments

by J. Richman

~~~

explicit sexual confession
by your lover
are power trips that inflict more pain
than enlightenment

Your Comments

by J. Richman

❧

unfortunately the "rush"
of a new lover felt is
often is addictive

Your Comments

by J. Richman

all excuses for betrayal
are inexcusable

_____

Your Comments

by J. Richman

∾∾∾

some know why they
are often wrong
yet can't get it right

_____

Your Comments

by J. Richman

⤙⤚

some people that have
a photographic memory
don't have a clue

Your Comments

the thing about attorneys
is they're so willingly trained
to ignore what's fair or right

Your Comments

179

by J. Richman

∽∾∽

it takes more than
praise to overcome
low self-esteem

_____

Your Comments

by J. Richman

⌐⌐⌐

my life is a series of overlapping
great adventures
but few of my conscious choosing

Your Comments

by J. Richman

∽∾∾

as time passes friends and lovers have
slipped off the edge of the world
I miss them

_____

Your Comments

by J. Richman

∽∼∾

the American Indian fought
for their simple life
the rest of us are too passive

Your Comments

183

by J. Richman

❧

in the ghetto
mother is only
half a word

_____

Your Comments

∽∾∽

we do much of what
we intend not to do

Your Comments

by J. Richman

❦

self-appointed victim
must expect to sacrifice
everything to it

Your Comments

186

〜〜

what is it that sets people
against themselves

Your Comments

187

∾⧸∾

what does it take to
jar a man loose from
his past held beliefs

_____

Your Comments

by J. Richman

∻∻∻

squaring the circle is easier than
changing your mate's character

Your Comments

by J. Richman

❧

geniuses and the insane
make connections
other minds don't make

_____

Your Comments

by J. Richman

❦

some people don't need a hand
throwing caution to the wind

Your Comments

191

by J. Richman

we want a beautiful lady
but we know down the line
it's character that will
override everything

_____

Your Comments

by J. Richman

❧❧

Remember to say
my love never stops
even when
I am angered by you

Your Comments

by J. Richman

⌒⌒⌒

don't let hurt feelings
and anger run together

Your Comments

∽∾∽

only parts of us can disappear

Your Comments

❧

I look at my grandfather's pictures
And now understand
what he knew about his place in time

_____

Your Comments

196

by J. Richman

❥❥

of babies and computers
junk in junk out

Your Comments

by J. Richman

while awake
how do I get back to that
place of bliss
I know waking from
an unrecalled dream

_____

Your Comments

by J. Richman

why do so few choose
a noble life

_____

Your Comments

〜〜

act noble- be noble
Could it work
give it a try

_____

Your Comments

200

can anyone spend too much time
in search of themselves

_____

Your Comments

by J. Richman

⌒⌒

non- attachment to your partner
while dancing or making love
lacks both passion and purpose

Your Comments

∽∽

to kill Indians
they killed the buffalo
put them on reservations
today think ghetto
drugs and prison
few escape

Your Comments

203

by J. Richman

❦

internet dating
where fantasy people
seek perfect people
unlike themselves

Your Comments

by J. Richman

⤟

nightclubs
like looking for
a mate in a bowl
of pariah

Your Comments

by J. Richman

❦

I miss sharing breath
on long kisses while
making love slowly to the
unknown woman who
haunts my dreams

_____

Your Comments

206

∾∾∾

75,000 homeless living
on the streets of Los Angele
and it is the best of times

_____

Your Comments

～～

life's fantasies are just that
some can settle for now
why can't I

_____

Your Comments

208

by J. Richman

∽∾∾

no cities reputation will ever exceed
it's poorest deplorable schools
what must those kids think of us

Your Comments

by J. Richman

༼ေၪ

the melting pot
has been replaced
by the pots of special interest

Your Comments

by J. Richman

⚬∾⚬

politicians promote BS harsh laws
to scare you into electing them

Your Comments

by J. Richman

❧

prohibition on booze
didn't work either
Because government against
its people always fails

_____

Your Comments

by J. Richman

∾∾∾

how can I explain to you or me
a feeling that now and then
some spirit is hugging me

Your Comments

by J. Richman

∽∾∽

the answer for past errors
is that was before I knew better

_____

Your Comments

❦

as I age
my herding instincts fade

Your Comments

by J. Richman

∽∾∽

as our deeds drop farther into
the shadows of the past
one can't help but wonder

_____

Your Comments

by J. Richman

❧❧❧

who do you ask advice from
foretells the answer

Your Comments

by J. Richman

⌒⌒

modern day fact
marriage and love forever or
until someone gets bored

_____

Your Comments

218

❦

don't only do those things
your fears will let you do

_____

Your Comments

by J. Richman

〜〜

name those things that you
would do if you had no fear
then do something about it

Your Comments

by J. Richman

∽∾∾

how do I explain to you and me
that two of the women I loved
were lesbian before and after

_____

Your Comments

by J. Richman

∽∼∾

I know I am ok with myself
when I am alone but not lonely

Your Comments

❧❧❧

beware of politicians who whip up
emotions to make us
suspicious of others unlike us

Your Comments

ᥫ᩠᠀᠊

as a elected city politician
I overestimated the public's enthusiasm
for enlightenment of government
corruption

Your Comments

by J. Richman

∽∾∽

there are times there is this sadness
that I never reached my potential
but then who has

Your Comments

by J. Richman

～⌇～

life is like a puzzle with
too many pieces

_____

Your Comments

by J. Richman

⌒⌒⌒

reputations good or bad
mostly reflect little truth

_____

Your Comments

people
are more interesting when
when they wear their passions
like a fine coat for all to see

Your Comments

by J. Richman

∾∾

a woman who doesn't
give her husband
emotional support will soon
be un-$upported

Your Comments

by J. Richman

❧

the violin requires and advanced
soul to play and other to enjoy

_____

Your Comments

by J. Richman

❧❦❧

I give comfort to my kids
friends and clients
but long for that mate that can
recharge my battery

Your Comments

231

by J. Richman

❧

what a great joy it would to hold
and be held by that unknown
special woman thru the night

_____

Your Comments

by J. Richman

∽⌒∼

sometimes I do not
take my own advise
and that was right

Your Comments

by J. Richman

⊶⊷

scolding other for bad deeds
and errors may feels good
but you will soon know
the taste of hate

Your Comments

෴

there are people hearing the
voice of God or the devil
asking do their bidding
they are all insane

_____

Your Comments

by J. Richman

❦

we all stumble
trying to find a
balanced life

Your Comments

by J. Richman

don't feel alone
we have all known the great
passions of
love, rage and loss

Your Comments

by J. Richman

∽⚬∾

new Lovers often
feels unequal
to the task

_____

Your Comments

by J. Richman

~∾~

swim hard to get
from point A or B
with life cross currents
often us to get to F

Your Comments

by J. Richman

if your obituary won't read
an amazing life and you
are alive
do something amazing

Your Comments

by J. Richman

~~

I don't live each day
as my last
as I would soon starve

_____

Your Comments

by J. Richman

❧

on your death bed
with life's work done
will you think oh crap
or well done

Your Comments

by J. Richman

do great deeds overshadow
great fault
not so much now

_____

Your Comments

by J. Richman

∽∾∽

when most men tell me of their life
I hear all but a noble purpose

_____

Your Comments

by J. Richman

⌒⌒

it is odd that degrees of happiness
find me each day
despite my misspent opportunities

_____

Your Comments

by J. Richman

❧

cold rational people with their control
avoid both great pain and joy

_____

Your Comments

by J. Richman

∽∾

there are rare moments never
repeated never forgotten
it's a magic moment when a youth
sees himself as a man

_____

Your Comments

by J. Richman

❦

when I'm finished
will the end also be a
complete surprise

Your Comments

❦

a trail of words is
often completely
different
same person

Your Comments

by J. Richman

❧

most men are affected by
the phantom of the opera
we have known his pain
those that haven't are still boys

Your Comments

250

⌒⌒⌒

my home is name
casa alamano
after an imagined place
where everything was just right
created by my 5 year old son

_____

Your Comments

251

᷉᷼᷍

there are thoughts
that should be written
then burnt and the ashes blown away
I have done that—

_____

Your Comments

by J. Richman

⌒⌒

I have been heroic and cowardly
down trotter and trodden
loved and hated
but we all—-have

Your Comments

by J. Richman

⌘

my Asian bride
bridged the internet
and 8,000 miles to
be by my side
neat 10 year story

Your Comments

by J. Richman

There is much to be
said for an
occasional lament

Your Comments

by J. Richman

❧

we often have sane ideas
but live in an insane world

_____

Your Comments

by J. Richman

⌐∽∽⌐

It is unsettling
to know only the past
of former loves

Your Comments

by J. Richman

❧

sometimes we are required
by our nature
to step aside
but it's not a good habit

Your Comments

by J. Richman

⤬⤬⤬

by our human nature
we have caused pain to
ourselves and others
forgive yourself
few others will

by J. Richman

∽⌒∽

we must touch someone
each day some way or
become touched in the head

_____

Your Comments

260

by J. Richman

⮑⮐

you can go home again
but it is a trip
only your mind can make

_____

Your Comments

by J. Richman

⌒⌒⌒

I want to do
yet unknown
brave deeds

_____

Your Comments

by J. Richman

we all have a place
deep inside
filled with regrets
known only to us

Your Comments

by J. Richman

❧

most women want a man
with a club
at the cave entrance

_____

Your Comments

by J. Richman

❦

too many believers seem to
think praying,
not doing is all that's required

Your Comments

by J. Richman

❦

as mighty as I try not to
treat different people
differently-but I do

Your Comments

by J. Richman

∽∾∽

If you are beside yourself
with anger
you're poor company

_____

Your Comments

by J. Richman

❦

life can be a problem for
those not used to letting
go of problems

_____

Your Comments

by J. Richman

〜〜

no one will really know us
unless of course you write
a book like this

Your Comments

by J. Richman

⌒⌒⌒

on an uneven flow
the times and loves
of my life come and go

Your Comments

by J. Richman

◆∾◆

if you don't like
your life's audience
change your act
or your audience

Your Comments

by J. Richman

⤳⤳

If you're not willing to
change anything
you better have a perfect life

_____

Your Comments

272

can a friendship ever turn
into a passionate love

Your Comments

by J. Richman

〜〜

It is unsettling that we
do not have an idea of
who we will become

Your Comments

❦

grandfather
age 3 sat on his lap
age 4 sat on his grave
I still miss him

Your Comments

by J. Richman

❦

what is it that pulls us
to some and not others

Your Comments

∽∾

I don't wish become a bore
and changes nothing

_____

Your Comments

by J. Richman

❧

If we live a very long time
the trick is not to outlive ourselves

_____

Your Comments

by J. Richman

సౌ

sometimes I like
the past more than
when I was there

Your Comments

by J. Richman

❧

the fight or flight Instinct is
slowed only by brighter minds
considering other alternatives

_____

Your Comments

by J. Richman

∽∾∽

great artists seem to be haunted
by demons of their choosing

_____

Your Comments

by J. Richman

∾∽∾

when I find myself out of my bounds
I learn much about pain and pleasure
a required trips to get anywhere

_____

Your Comments

by J. Richman

ᑌᑌᑌ

the problem with getting
older but looking younger
is I don't fit in any group

Your Comments

by J. Richman

❧

the problem with having
been with to many ladies
you come to know that

Your Comments

by J. Richman

∽∼∾

the old question of
half a glass of water
misses the real question
is the water
rising or falling

Your Comments

by J. Richman

〜〜〜

there are no
ordinary anything
only seems that way
if you don't
pay attention

Your Comments

286

by J. Richman

❧

I will not soon
be my best self

Your Comments

∾

when parts of life
are falling apart
sometimes it is best
not pick up the pieces

Your Comments

by J. Richman

logical thinking
is not compatible
with magical hoping

Your Comments

by J. Richman

∾∾∾

the idea that all
problems have solutions
is a product of nonsense

Your Comments

by J. Richman

෴

shedding illusions
gathered each day
every year is a
full time job

Your Comments

by J. Richman

⤳⤳⤳

as I got closer to potential friends
and lovers, and far way places
I often realized the distant view
was best.

_____

Your Comments

292

∾∾∾

we all have not only the right
but the duty to escape from being
less than what we want to be—
therefore need to be.

_____

Your Comments

by J. Richman

꙰

I know I will regret the dumb
things I will do in the future
question is when can I
get smarter

Your Comments

by J. Richman

∽∾

married women out with the girls
in a bar filled with singles is a lot
like their husbands in a whore house
with a fist full hundreds
it is just a matter of time

Your Comments

࿐

If you need a alarm clock to
wake up—
then wake that something
is wrong is your life

_____

Your Comments

by J. Richman

c␣␣

in order read good news
these days we must read the
obituaries for a story about a
successful life

Your Comments

by J. Richman

❦

I am impressed when the
frail fight for their rights.

Your Comments

by J. Richman

∽∼∽

digging in my life's trash
is a learning experience
best not done often

_____

Your Comments

by J. Richman

❦

for a women the question is
one hour one night one year
one life time

Your Comments

by J. Richman

ꭟꭏꭏ

there are things
about our lives
we do not ever
want to hear.

Your Comments

by J. Richman

❧

there no cheers
for civilization as
this is not yet a
civil world

Your Comments

mother nature
a poor name
mothers nature
doesn't care

Your Comments

303

by J. Richman

❧

now and then there
is this sadness of what
could if been

_____

Your Comments

by J. Richman

~~~

Hmmm so much is
not the same now

Your Comments

by J. Richman

～∾～

once we are well fed and
have a warm safe bed
we need justice

_____

Your Comments

by J. Richman

⌒⌒⌒

something to ponder
symphony orchestras are a
collect of very odd looking
people collectively making
something beautiful

Your Comments

by J. Richman

⤳⤳

completly satisfied with
your life
Hmmmm
You are easily satisfied

Your Comments

by J. Richman

I still miss the father
I never knew—I often
wonder would I be
different

Your Comments

by J. Richman

⌒⌒⌒

A great marriage requires
a great friendship
great sex appeal is not
enough in the long run

Your Comments

ᴄᴀᴄᴀᴏ

Sex as a sport with a team
of players works for
only a while

_____

Your Comments

by J. Richman

❦

Every time I look in the mirror
I expect to see a younger man

Your Comments

by J. Richman

❧❧

If someone states
it is not personal
it is

Your Comments

∽∾

there are homeless people
that will not give up
drugs, booze and
freedom
in order to qualify for
government housing

Your Comments

by J. Richman

❦

holding emotions in check
is ok except when
showing affection

_____

Your Comments

by J. Richman

❧

once opening the door to
bitching
it is very hard to shut

Your Comments

∾⌇∾

our possibility to recall past love
fads making possibility
the next romance

Your Comments

by J. Richman

❧

it is hard to hear I am
unqualified by a
lover even if I know
know she is wrong
===still there a lost

Your Comments

by J. Richman

೧౨౭

holding emotion in check
Is normally ok———
but there are times——-
you could miss a good times

Your Comments

by J. Richman

୰୰

Your roommate is a gorilla
bucket food in crap out
it escapes the chains
oddly you will miss the
companionship

Your Comments

by J. Richman

࿐

at 98 mother became a
stranger to her life
sorry mom I did not
handle that well.

Your Comments

⌘

men know the different
between
let him and want him
some men don't care.

_____

Your Comments

by J. Richman

~~~

if "me too" was started in
the 1700 the founders
would of be replaced by
Mr. milk toast and defeat

Your Comments

by J. Richman

❧

there was never a time I
didn't consider that different
people could bring out a
crappy side of me.

Your Comments

by J. Richman

〜〜〜

sorry some people
are not repairable

Your Comments

by J. Richman

❧

how long can our
loneliness be lost
in a wrong embrace

Your Comments

by J. Richman

∿

your life's plan is
voluntary don't
make it involuntary

Your Comments

by J. Richman

⚭

odd many life's rules were made
by long ago dead that dressed
in outlandish robes and silly hats

_____

Your Comments

by J. Richman

❦

somethings
drive me crazy
I have arrived

Your Comments

~~~

enough
every had enough
how long did
enough stay enough

Your Comments

by J. Richman

∾

for most wives
experts live
far away

_____

Your Comments

331

by J. Richman

～～

emotions
to little a bore
to much crazy
just right rare

_____

Your Comments

332

by J. Richman

☙❦❧

some women I have been
with tried to change me lot
if successful
would they hated or loved me

_____

Your Comments

333

what would happen if I pretend
for 48 hours I am not me and
be who I want to be.

Your Comments

one lady I loved 365 nights
one lady I only loved 300 days
problem same women

Your Comments

by J. Richman

⚬⚬⚬

as I get older
I forgot some of my errors
then some sob
remind me and the world

Your Comments

by J. Richman

꧁

be careful
easy to mistake
friendliness for friendship

Your Comments

note if someone laughs way
to much at any little joke
step away

Your Comments

by J. Richman

∾∾

seems nothing I do that is
important is easy nor quick

Your Comments

by J. Richman

❧

hard lesson
she seems irresistible but
she dose not have enough
of "it' that you need her to
give or have——— move on

Your Comments

∽∾∽

given when we think
we could of or should of
accomplished—
there a sadness
so do not go there often

Your Comments

by J. Richman

⌒⌒

we all would like to be known
to others as a safe place
on cold story times

_____

Your Comments

by J. Richman

࿇

greedy people could get it all
and never have enough

_____

Your Comments

by J. Richman

❧

best not to be with a lady
that is often controlled
by ill conceived first impulse
they can be exciting but freighting

_____

Your Comments

by J. Richman

❧❧

got to be dumb to believe the
1000s silly reasons given why
stocks go up or down..
think commission on sales

_____

Your Comments

∽∾∽

no one react well to all thing
all the time
do not be too hard on yourself

_____

Your Comments

by J. Richman

∾

accepting people unlike me
is still a step by step process
logic fighting old emotions

Your Comments

by J. Richman

~~~

home is so much more
that a house

_____

Your Comments

by J. Richman

❦

a soulmate is a dumb term
think 1000s of them for you
still hard to find

_____

Your Comments

⌒⌒

know us by our enemies
Hustler prono magazine named me
asshole of the month for stopping
drug infested concerts in Burbank
30 years later I am still proud of that

_____

Your Comments

∽⚬∾

sober or Jim beam thoughts
in the hot tub
big differences next day

_____

Your Comments

351

by J. Richman

❧

time is on my side—nice song
however
do not count on that

Your Comments

by J. Richman

∽∼∾

when in political office
a dud bomb planted
by my bedroom did not stop
me from exposing the sobs.
not sure why—-seems I got very mad

Your Comments

by J. Richman

෴

as I got older I thought I would lose
interest in romance——silly me

Your Comments

by J. Richman

⌒⌒⌒

do not let time abuse you
use time while you got time.

Your Comments

by J. Richman

༄༅

I grew up like a
untended wild a weed
but changed by forced by the
changing weathers of my life
I am about even
errors and accomplishments

Your Comments

by J. Richman